THE LIFE OF PAUL

Rose Visual
Bible Studies

The Life of Paul
Rose Visual Bible Studies

©2018 Rose Publishing, LLC

Rose Publishing, LLC
P.O. Box 3473
Peabody, Massachusetts 01961-3473 USA
www.hendricksonrose.com

Author: Carl Simmons

Book design by Cristalle Kishi.

Images used under license from Shutterstock.com and Lightstock, LLC.

Printed in the United States of America
010418VP

Contents

"I can do all things through Christ who strengthens me."

The apostle Paul,
Philippians 4:13 NKJV

The Life of Paul

As we travel through the New Testament book of Acts, we see the incredible story of Paul, a man who went from being a virulent persecutor *of* Christians to being repeatedly persecuted *for* being a Christian himself.

We see a man who faced hostile crowds of pagans and devout Jews alike in order to spread the gospel of Jesus. We see him vehemently opposing heretics who tried to twist the gospel, as well as disciplining Christians who weren't living up to *their* faith—sometimes gently, sometimes not so gently. At the same time, we see him encouraging those he worked with and suffered alongside for their faith "like a father with his children" (1 Thessalonians 2:11 ESV). Throughout all this, we see a man who planted and nurtured young churches from Greece to Asia Minor in locations hostile to the power of the gospel.

In short, we see a man who happily said, "I consider everything a loss because of the surpassing worth of knowing Christ Jesus my Lord, for whose sake I have lost all things. I consider them garbage, that I may gain Christ" (Philippians 3:8).

In the six sessions of this Bible study, you'll read and reflect on key Bible passages about Paul's life and mission. If you read the *Optional Reading* Bible passages for all six sessions, by the end of this study, you will have read the entire life of Paul in the book of Acts, as well as some important passages in Paul's letters.

As you see Paul in all the phases and circumstances of his life, hopefully you'll recognize yourself as well—and, more importantly, you'll recognize who you are in Christ—and be inspired by the amazing things God did through the life and character of this man named Paul.

PAUL'S UNEXPECTED JOURNEY

On the Road to Damascus

ACTS 9:1–22

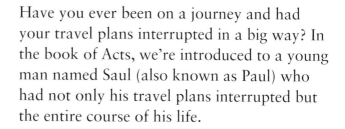

Have you ever been on a journey and had your travel plans interrupted in a big way? In the book of Acts, we're introduced to a young man named Saul (also known as Paul) who had not only his travel plans interrupted but the entire course of his life.

But first, here's the setting. Jesus has risen from the dead, and he gives his disciples a bold mission: "Be my witnesses in Jerusalem, and in all Judea and Samaria, and to the ends of the earth" (Acts 1:8). Jesus ascends to heaven. The disciples receive the Holy Spirit at Pentecost, and 3,000 people are baptized. The church has begun.

Peter, John, and Stephen are testifying publicly about the good news of Jesus. But not everyone in Jerusalem is pleased with this strange new movement. The city's leaders rile up a crowd, drag Stephen outside the city, and brutally kill him with stones.

Enter Saul. The people "laid their coats at the feet of a young man named Saul" (7:58) as Saul looked on approvingly at Stephen's execution. Yet Saul was determined not to remain just an onlooker. "Saul began to destroy the church. Going from house to house, he dragged off both men and women and put them in prison" (8:3). Saul had plans for the complete destruction of the church. But God had other plans for him.

Read It

Key Bible Passage

For this session, read Acts 9:1–22.

Optional Reading

Acts 7:54–8:3; Galatians 1:11–18; Philippians 3:3–11

This extra reading covers Paul's role in the execution of Stephen and more about Paul's background.

"He fell to the ground and heard a voice say to him, 'Saul, Saul, why do you persecute me?'"

ACTS 9:4

Know It

1. Where was Saul going at the beginning of this passage, and why? What do his actions reveal about him?

   To the synagogue in Damascus to persecute Christians.

   He was zealous for Judaism & wanted to completely destroy the church.

2. How might you have responded if you'd been in Ananias's place knowing what you already knew about Saul?

   Very afraid & reluctant to go anywhere near Saul.

3. What was Saul doing at the end of this narrative? What had clearly changed about him?

   He was filled with the Holy Spirit

   He was preaching that Jesus is the son of God

Explore It

Paul's Background

Paul (also known as Saul) was born in Tarsus (in modern-day Turkey), probably sometime between AD 2 and 5. Tarsus was a cosmopolitan port city known for its wealth and privilege. Years later, in one of his letters, Paul describes himself as having been "of the people of Israel, of the tribe of Benjamin, a Hebrew of Hebrews" (Philippians 3:5). Although Paul was an Israelite, he was also a citizen of the Roman Empire by birth. This dual citizenship would later serve him well in both his life and ministry (Acts 22:25–29; 25:10–12).

While still in his youth, Paul came to Jerusalem where he studied under Gamaliel, the famous Jewish teacher (Acts 22:3; 5:34). Gamaliel was probably a senior member of the Sanhedrin (council) and may have even been its chief member at one time. He was also a chief figure among the Pharisees, who were known for their strict observance of both Mosaic and traditional law. The Pharisees would also become famous for their hypocrisy, as they often enforced standards they refused to keep themselves—something Jesus called them out on regularly (Matthew 6:1–5; 23:1–12; Luke 11:37–52).

Nonetheless, Gamaliel had helped save the lives of early Christians. In Acts 5, the apostles John and Peter stood trial before the Sanhedrin for preaching the name of Jesus. Gamaliel addressed the Sanhedrin, reminding them of past insurrectionists, then warned the council: "Leave these men alone! Let them go! For if their purpose or activity is of human origin, it will fail. But if it is from God, you will not be able to stop these men; you will only find yourselves fighting against God" (Acts 5:38–39). As a result, John and Peter were freed—and "never stopped teaching and proclaiming the good news that Jesus is the Messiah" (5:42).

Gamaliel's pupil, Paul, however, chose a very different path. Paul became fanatical in defense of his Jewish faith against the followers of Jesus. Paul was present at the stoning of the first Christian martyr, Stephen, and looked on approvingly. He then persecuted the church throughout Jerusalem (Acts 7:54–8:3; Galatians 1:13–14).

Despite his religious zeal, he was blind to whom Jesus really was—the God he so fervently desired to serve. Paul would look back on this period of his life and say:

> I persecuted the church of God and tried to destroy it. I was advancing in Judaism beyond many of my own age among my people and was extremely zealous for the traditions of my fathers (Galatians 1:13–14).

Paul's religious ambitions against the disciples of Jesus took him beyond Jerusalem, north toward the city of Damascus.

| AD 5 | 10 | 15 | 20 |

◆ Paul is born, an Israelite from the tribe of Benjamin and a Roman citizen by birth. He is raised in Tarsus of Cilicia and given the Hebrew name of Saul. **AD 5**

Paul receives a privileged education, studying under the Jewish scholar Gamaliel. **AD 10–30**

Caesar Augustus rules the Roman Empire. **27 BC–AD 14**

Emperor Tiberius rules the Roman Empire. **AD 14–37**

Herod Antipas governs Galilee. **4 BC–AD 39**

(Dates are approximate.)

Journey to Damascus

Although the church in Damascus certainly had been formed by the time Paul traveled to the city, there is reason to believe that there were believers there even while Jesus was still on earth. As the capital of Syria and the oldest inhabited city in the world—and given its proximity to Jerusalem, about 130 miles (209 km) to the northeast—it's not surprising that the city of Damascus would be an early stronghold for the church. It would also not be a huge surprise, then, that after persecuting the church in Jerusalem, Paul would next set his sights on Damascus. Moreover, it's possible that some of the Christians in Jerusalem may have fled to Damascus to escape persecution. Paul may have also been heading to Damascus to bring back those refugees to face punishment in Jerusalem.

Paul set out for Damascus to apprehend followers of Jesus, but on the way, it was he who was "apprehended by Christ Jesus" (Philippians 3:12 KJV). A great light flashed from heaven, Paul fell to the ground, and the risen Jesus revealed the truth to Paul: "I am

25	30	35	40

Jesus is crucified in Jerusalem. He is raised from the dead, appears to many, and ascends to heaven. AD 30

Jesus' disciples receive the Holy Spirit in Jerusalem on Pentecost. AD 30

Stephen is martyred in Jerusalem. Paul looks on approvingly. AD 32

Paul persecutes believers in Jesus. AD 32–37

Paul encounters Jesus on the road to Damascus. He becomes a believer and is baptized. AD 37

Pontius Pilate governs Judea. AD 26–36

Paul begins to preach the good news of Jesus in synagogues. AD 37

Jesus, whom you are persecuting" (Acts 9:5). Physically blinded by the experience, Paul arrived in Damascus where the Lord directed a Christian named Ananias to go to Paul and restore his sight. While Paul's physical sight was restored, it was really his spiritual sight that made all the difference. Paul would go on to become a force that influenced the world for God *as* a disciple of Jesus. Years later, he would write this about both his old life and his new life:

> In regard to the law, [I was] a Pharisee; as for zeal, persecuting the church; as for righteousness based on the law, faultless. But whatever were gains to me I now consider loss for the sake of Christ. What is more, I consider everything a loss because of the surpassing worth of knowing Christ Jesus my Lord, for whose sake I have lost all things. I consider them garbage, that I may gain Christ (Philippians 3:5–8).

Paul Before and After His Encounter with Jesus

BEFORE	AFTER
Approved of the murder of a Christian man named Stephen (Acts 8:1)	Accepted the help of a Christian man named Ananias (Acts 9:17)
"Breathed out murderous threats against the Lord's disciples" (Acts 9:1)	Preached "that Jesus is the Son of God" (Acts 9:20)
Sought out synagogues to get approval, so he could persecute followers of Jesus (Acts 9:1–2)	Went to the synagogues to prove "that Jesus is the Messiah" (Acts 9:20, 22)

Saul or Paul?

Although other biblical examples of name changes (Abram to Abraham, Jacob to Israel) make it easy to think that Jesus changed Saul's name to Paul on the road to Damascus, the most likely explanation is probably less dramatic.

We read the name Paul for the first time in Acts 13:9 ("Saul, who was also called Paul"), more than a decade after the events of Acts 9. It is likely that the dual names Saul and Paul were reflective of the apostle's dual heritage as a Hebrew and a Roman: Saul his Hebrew name, and Paul his Roman (or Gentile) name. In addition, the first use of the name Paul in Acts occurs on Cyprus, where he leads the Roman proconsul Sergius Paulus to Christ (13:7–12). As it became increasingly obvious that Paul's mission was to the Gentiles, he would use his Gentile name more frequently as he traveled further into the Gentile world.

Live It

You may not have actively persecuted Christians as Paul did, but as Paul would write years after this event, we have *all* been enemies of Christ. Just as with Paul, it takes an encounter with the risen Jesus to change that.

> For if, while we were God's enemies, we were reconciled to him through the death of his Son, how much more, having been reconciled, shall we be saved through his life! Not only is this so, but we also boast in God through our Lord Jesus Christ, through whom we have now received reconciliation (Romans 5:10–11).

Knowing Jesus changes our standing before God, the direction of our lives, the way we use the gifts God has given us, our purpose in life . . . everything.

Many believe that Jesus' transfiguration took place at or near Mount Hermon, only about 25 miles (40 km) from Damascus—and which can actually be seen from the road to Damascus Paul traveled in Acts 9.

Life Application Questions

1. How has your life journey been changed or been *unexpected* because you know Jesus?

   I know that I can get thru anything with Jesus by my side - pain, loss, death + know that we will all be together at the end in heaven

2. Paul thought he was doing God's will by going after Christians, but his encounter with Jesus showed him how wrong he was. How would you feel if you found out that the good things you thought you were doing for Christ were hurtful to him instead? Have you ever experienced this?

   I would feel terrible, horrified, ashamed

3. When has God used a situation or revelation to convict you of sin or to show you how you were on the wrong path in life?

   thru pain + a leave from work. thru Tyler

4. After his conversion, Paul met with the very people he had tried to destroy and he preached the gospel to those who had helped him persecute believers. How have you seen relationships between people be radically changed because of a relationship with Jesus?

5. Paul had a lot of seemingly positive qualities (zeal, religious education, etc.), but he had greatly misused them. How have you seen God redirect talents, resources, or personality traits to be used for good instead of evil?

6. Paul had been blind to what God really wanted him to do. Where does it feel like the scales still need to fall from your eyes, so you can clearly see what God wants you to do?

- With outside my community
- With Adam + family

Prayer

Lord, thank you for all you've done in our lives. We thank you that you've allowed us to know you. More importantly, we thank you for knowing us, and creating and saving us for your purposes. Help us to develop a deeper appreciation of everything you've done in our lives, and give us the ability and desire to let our light shine before others. In Jesus' name, amen.

This Coming Week

Consider the following options for living out your faith in response to this session's study—or come up with one of your own. Then, *do it*.

- Where have you encountered Jesus in the past? Your church? A mountaintop? Your kitchen? If possible, go there this week. Reflect on how knowing Jesus has changed your own life, and spend some time thanking him for it. Then share with someone what you've experienced.

- Get together with a friend this week, and share what God has done in your life. You could share your testimony of how Jesus has changed you or tell about how God helped you through a situation similar to one your friend might be facing now. Do more than just talk, though; listen for opportunities to encourage and pray for your friend.

Notes

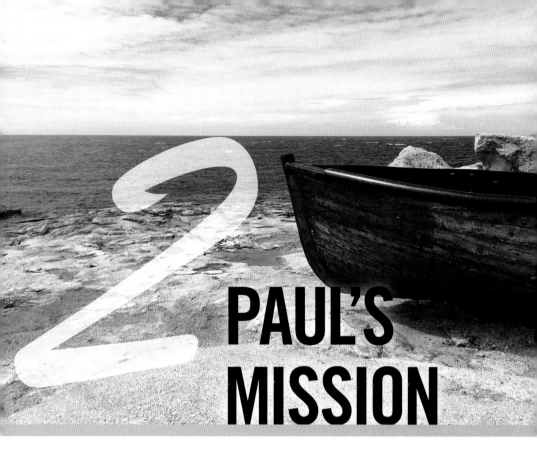

2

PAUL'S MISSION

*Called to Proclaim
the Gospel*

ACTS 12:25–13:52

When have you known you were just *meant* to do something? For that matter, have you ever done something knowing that it was *God* calling you to do it—and that's what kept you going when things got tough?

Paul had a calling from God. His own goal *had been* to put an end to the gospel of Jesus, but his mission *became* to spread the gospel to the world. In his letter to the Galatians, Paul would remind believers:

> Even before I was born, God chose me and called me by his marvelous grace. Then it pleased him to reveal his Son to me so that I would proclaim the Good News about Jesus to the Gentiles (Galatians 1:15–16 NLT).

In this session's Bible reading, we'll see how the Holy Spirit moved Paul and other believers to advance the mission God had given them— even in the face of fierce opposition.

Read It

Key Bible Passage

For this session, read Acts 12:25–13:52.

Optional Reading

Acts 9:23–31; 11:19–30; 12:25–14:28

This extra reading covers from Paul's escape from Damascus through the end of his first missionary journey. (It also includes the *Key Bible Passage* for this session.)

> "The Holy Spirit said, 'Set apart for me Barnabas and Saul for the work to which I have called them.'"
>
> **ACTS 13:2**

Know It

1. Who called Paul and Barnabas to their mission? What do the prophets and teachers at Antioch do in response?

   The Holy Spirit called them to their mission.

   The prophets + teachers fasted + prayed + laid hands on them.

2. Imagine being John Mark. What might you have thought and felt as you traveled with Paul and Barnabas? As you watched them confront Elymas? As you left them and went back home?

   Wide-eyed with amazement at what Paul + Barnabas could do by influencing people in the name of God. Blinding Elymas. The number of people who's lives they changed.

3. Who do you identify with most in this story? Why?

   ❏ Paul—filled with the Spirit

   ❏ Barnabas—set apart by God along with Paul

   ❏ John Mark—the helper who didn't stay long

   ❏ Elymas—opposed the gospel

   ❏ Sergius Paulus—amazed by what God was doing

   ❏ The synagogue leaders—jealous and angry

   ☑ The Gentiles—honored that God's Word was for them as well

Paul's "Lost" Years

Nearly ten years passed between Paul's encounter with Jesus on the road to Damascus and the start of Paul's first formal missionary journey. The book of Acts is silent about much of this time, but we do gain some insight into this "lost" period from Paul's letter to the Galatians.

Based on this letter, it would appear that Paul did not go to Jerusalem immediately after escaping a plot against his life in Damascus (Acts 9:23–26)—in fact, three years would pass. Paul first went to Arabia, then returned to Damascus (Galatians 1:15–18). It is likely that Paul preached in Arabia as well, even though King Aretas IV of Nabatæan (northern) Arabia had been part of the conspiracy to seize Paul in Damascus (2 Corinthians 11:32–33). Aretas's actions were likely motivated by the fact that he was the father-in-law of King Herod Antipas, who governed Galilee during Jesus' time and whose death was graphically portrayed in Acts 12:20–23.

After Paul's time in Arabia and Damascus, he then went to Jerusalem. But he was not yet fully trusted by the leaders of the early church:

> When he came to Jerusalem, he tried to join the disciples, but they were all afraid of him, not believing that he really was a disciple (Acts 9:26).

It is at this point that Barnabas becomes a major figure in the book of Acts. We were introduced to him in Acts 4:36 as Joseph, nicknamed Barnabas (or "son of encouragement"), a Levite from Cyprus. Barnabas had sold a field and laid the money "at the apostlestt feet" (4:37) so that the funds could be distributed among the poor. In Acts 9, he stood up for Paul, recounting all that had happened to Paul on the road to Damascus and "how at Damascus [Paul] had preached fearlessly in the name of Jesus" (9:27). With Barnabas advocating for him, Paul was finally accepted.

Sometime during this period, Paul stayed with the apostle Peter for fifteen days and also met with Jesus' half-brother James (Galatians 1:18–19).

Paul went on to preach in Jerusalem, and once again, he received death threats and was compelled to escape, first to Caesarea and ultimately to his hometown of Tarsus (Acts 9:28–30). At this point, the biblical account goes silent for several years. All we know about this time comes from Paul's account in his letter to the

| AD 37 | 38 | 39 | 40 | 41 | 42 | 43 |

◆ A plot against Paul's life forces him to escape from Damascus; he's lowered in a basket through an opening in the city wall. **AD 37**

Paul spends about three years in Arabia, then returns to Damascus. **AD 37–40**

◆ God calls Peter to bring the gospel message to a centurion named Cornelius, a Gentile. **AD 40**

◆ Paul goes to Jerusalem, but the Christians there are suspicious of him. With the help of Barnabas, they accept him into the congregation. Eventually, another plot against his life forces him to flee Jerusalem for Caesarea, then later to Tarsus. **AD 40**

Caligula rules the Roman Empire. **AD 37–41**

◆ Claudius assassinates Caligula to become the emperor. **AD 41**

Galatians where he wrote that the apostles only heard the report: "The man who formerly persecuted us is now preaching the faith he once tried to destroy" (Galatians 1:23).

The account of Paul's life picks up again in Acts 11, after men from Cyprus and Cyrene preached to the Gentiles in Antioch of Syria, and as a result "a great number of people believed and turned to the Lord" (11:21). The Jerusalem church sent Barnabas to Antioch. Barnabas, in turn, fetched Paul from Tarsus and "for a whole year Barnabas and Saul met with the church and taught great numbers of people. The disciples were called Christians first at Antioch" (11:26).

During this time, a great famine was predicted in Jerusalem. The church in Antioch determined to send relief. The other believers apparently trusted Barnabas and Paul immensely because they gave them the responsibility of delivering the funds they had collected for those in need in Jerusalem. It is this "service" (or "mission") that is referred to in Acts 12:25.

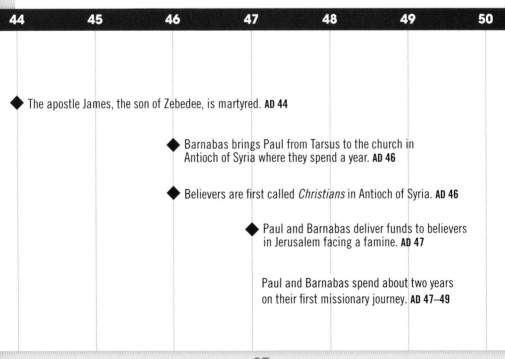

| 44 | 45 | 46 | 47 | 48 | 49 | 50 |

◆ The apostle James, the son of Zebedee, is martyred. **AD 44**

◆ Barnabas brings Paul from Tarsus to the church in Antioch of Syria where they spend a year. **AD 46**

◆ Believers are first called *Christians* in Antioch of Syria. **AD 46**

◆ Paul and Barnabas deliver funds to believers in Jerusalem facing a famine. **AD 47**

Paul and Barnabas spend about two years on their first missionary journey. **AD 47–49**

PAUL'S FIRST MISSIONARY JOURNEY
AD 47–49; Acts 13:1–14:28

Travelers: Paul, Barnabas, John Mark

Main Route: Cyprus and Asia Minor (1,400 mi; 2,253 km)

1. **Antioch of Syria, Seleucia:** The Holy Spirit sends Paul and Barnabas to be missionaries. John Mark goes along as their helper.

2. **Salamis, Paphos:** Paul confronts a sorcerer named Elymas and blinds him.

3. **Perga:** John Mark leaves the group and returns to Jerusalem.

4. **Antioch of Pisidia:** Paul preaches his longest recorded sermon, and many become believers. Jewish leaders drive Paul and Barnabas out of the city. The Lord calls Paul to focus his ministry on Gentiles. The Gentiles are glad and many become believers.

5. **Iconium:** More plots against their lives force them to flee.

6. **Lystra:** When Paul heals a lame man, the townspeople think he and Barnabas are Greek gods. Jews from Antioch and Iconium stir up the crowd, and Paul is stoned and left for dead outside the city. But Paul survives and goes back into the city.

7. **Derbe:** Paul preaches and many disciples are added to the church.

8. **Lystra, Iconium, Antioch of Pisidia, Perga, Attalia:** On the return trip, Paul and Barnabas appoint elders in the churches they had planted.

9. **Antioch of Syria:** Paul and Barnabas remain here for a while, reporting what God had done. (Paul may have written his letter to the Galatians from here.)

Assos
Mitylene
MYSIA
ASIA
LYCAONIA
Chios
PHRYGIA
CILICIA
Ephesus
Samos
Antioch
Iconium
Derbe
Patmos
PISIDIA
Lystra
Tarsus
Antioch
Cos
Attalia
Perga
Seleucia
Cnidus
LYCIA
PAMPHYLIA
SYRIA
Patara
Myra
RHODES
CYPRUS
Salamis
CRETE
Salmone
Paphos
Damascus
Lasea
PHOENICIA
Sidon
Tyre
Mediterranean
Sea
GALILEE
Ptolemais
Caesarea
SAMARIA
Antipatris
Amman
Joppa
Jerusalem
JUDEA
Gaza

In the first century AD, Antioch of Syria became a major center of Christianity, second only to Jerusalem. It was the city from which Paul and Barnabas launched their first missionary journey. Today the city Antakya, Turkey, covers most of what was Antioch.

A Sorcerer, a Governor, and the Gospel

Paul's first stop on his first formal missionary journey was the island of Cyprus, where he visited two places: Salamis and Paphos.

In the city of Salamis, Paul and Barnabas began preaching in the synagogues, as was Paul's custom, especially since there were very few established churches early in his ministry. In contrast to later accounts in Acts, there is no mention of anyone responding to Paul's message—possibly because no one did.

Upon arriving in Paphos, they encountered a sorcerer named Bar-Jesus, or Elymas in Arabic, who apparently was an advisor to the governor (proconsul) Sergius Paulus. Given the governor's response later in this chapter and the fact that the sorcerer was Jewish, it may well have been that governor already had some

Tombs of the Kings at Paphos, Cyprus

interest in the Scriptures. But instead of blinding the governor to the faith as he had intended (Acts 13:8), the sorcerer himself was blinded when Paul pronounced judgment upon him. As a result, the governor's own spiritual blindness was lifted, and he believed in the Lord.

When he arrived in Antioch of Pisidia, Paul again started by preaching in the synagogue. This time a response is mentioned, and it would become a familiar pattern for Paul and those with him: both Jews and especially Gentiles would believe in Christ, but some Jews (often those in leadership) would become jealous and stir up persecution. These persecutors in Antioch succeeded in driving out Paul and Barnabas, but the apostles were unfazed; "they shook the dust off their feet as a warning to them and went to Iconium" (Acts 13:51).

This pattern we see throughout Paul's missionary journeys:

- Some people believe the gospel message.

- Some dismiss or ignore it.

- Some outright oppose it.

But Paul's mission—as is all believers' mission—was to testify about the good news of Jesus Christ. Whether the people's spiritual blindness was lifted was up to God. Paul's mission was to persevere, to press on with the calling God had given him. As Paul would write many years later to a young pastor named Timothy:

> Do not be ashamed of the testimony about our Lord or of me his prisoner. Rather, join with me in suffering for the gospel, by the power of God. He has saved us and called us to a holy life not because of anything we have done but because of his own purpose and grace (2 Timothy 1:8–9).

The Curious Case of John Mark

"John, also called Mark" (Acts 12:25) was a cousin of Barnabas (Colossians 4:10). He is traditionally believed to be the same Mark who wrote of the Gospel of Mark and was one of Peter's disciples.

It may have been cousin Barnabas's connection to Cyprus that enabled (and ennobled) John Mark to start the trip with Barnabas and Paul. We are not told exactly why John Mark left shortly into the trip, but it is clear from later passages that Paul felt that John Mark had abandoned them, which would later lead to Paul and Barnabas parting ways (Acts 15:37–40).

Fortunately, the story doesn't end there for John Mark—or Paul, for that matter. John Mark would later return with Barnabas to Cyprus (15:39). Years after Barnabas had given him this second chance (much as Barnabas had done for Paul years earlier), John Mark would help Paul regularly during his imprisonment in Rome, and Paul would commend him to the Colossian church (Colossians 4:10). Paul would be even more complimentary in his final letter to Timothy: "Get Mark and bring him with you, because he is helpful to me in my ministry" (2 Timothy 4:11).

Mark is a wonderful example to us today that failure need not be the end of the story. God can, and will, use us when we're truly ready.

It can be easy to romanticize the idea of "being called," or to think that it's only the domain of pastors and missionaries. But the fact is that God calls each of us to his work, big *and* small. It also means keeping in mind that no matter what the size of the task, the work God calls us to is bigger than us. It requires God's power, wisdom, and strength to complete.

Whether we sense a specific calling from God or not, we know that God has called us to live a new and different life in Christ.

- "I urge you to live a life worthy of the calling you have received" (Ephesians 4:1).

- "For God did not call us to be impure, but to live a holy life" (1 Thessalonians 4:7).

Paul and Barnabas show us that as we live out our new lives in Christ, God will entrust us with more and more.

Life Application Questions

1. Who is the most "called" person you know? How do you see this person live out his or her calling?

2. How can someone figure out what God's calling is for his or her life?

3. What things are you doing right now that you know God clearly has led you into, and how well are you doing with them?

4. Paul eventually forgave John Mark for leaving them—but not before it caused division between him and Barnabas. When have you faced a situation in which someone you depended on bailed out on you? How did you deal with it? Are there any unresolved issues you might still need to address with that person?

5. What opposition or challenges do you face in sharing and living out your faith in Christ that you feel could "take you down" if you let them?

6. How can you address those challenges to your faith? Who can help you?

Prayer

Lord, you've given each of us a meaningful calling, even if we don't realize it or know all the details yet. What we do know is that it's too big to accomplish on our own. We need you to help us to fulfill the work you've called us to. Give us the will to want to fulfill our calling; the energy, strength, and courage to accomplish it; and the gratitude to thank you for what you've done through us. In Jesus' name, amen.

This Coming Week

Consider the following options for living out your faith in response to this session's study—or come up with one of your own. Then, *do it.*

- Think some more about this week's life application questions. Thank God for what he has already led you through, and consider where God might be leading next— and what might be preventing you from taking that next step. If it would be helpful (and it probably would), get together with a Christian friend this week to talk and pray through your thoughts, visions, and dreams—as well as your fears and other roadblocks.

- The church at Antioch worshiped and fasted before sending out Barnabas and Paul (Acts 13:3), and Barnabas and Paul did the same as they commissioned elders in all the churches they visited (14:23). Consider skipping one meal a day for set period of time. Use your mealtime as a prayer and worship time instead. Maybe also donate the money you would have spent on your meal to a hunger-relief organization or a missionary from your church. (Before you begin fasting, check with your doctor. Your doctor is a key component in helping you find a good strategy for accomplishing your fast.)

3
PAUL'S SHARP DISPUTE

The Jerusalem Council

ACTS 15:1–35

Paul's Sharp Dispute

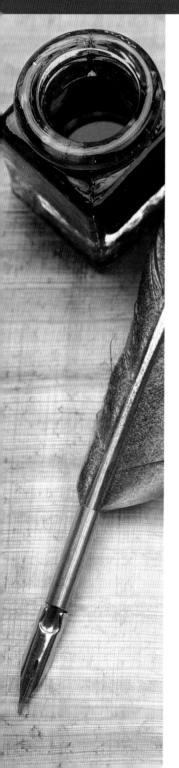

Have you ever been in the middle of an argument where everyone seemed to have a point or, worse yet, one where one side was clearly in the wrong and wouldn't back down? Paul and the apostles faced a crisis like this during the early life of the church—one that cut to the very core of who Jesus is and what he came to do.

At this point in Paul's story, he had concluded his first missionary journey where it began—in Antioch of Syria. Here, Paul and Barnabas reported to believers the wonderful news from their journey of how God "had opened a door of faith to the Gentiles" (Acts 14:27). This influx of Gentile Christians into newly growing churches—which had been largely composed of Jewish Christians—created a "sharp dispute" (15:2). This dispute required everyone involved to come to a peaceful resolution and still stay true to Jesus in the process.

Thankfully, they not only resolved this crisis, but in doing so, they gave us crucial insight into what it means and looks like to live and behave as Christians today as we face disputes in our churches.

Read It

Key Bible Passage

For this session, read Acts 15:1–35.

Optional Reading

Galatians 1:6–10; 3:1–14

This extra reading is from Paul's letter to churches in Galatia and deals with their problem of a false gospel spreading among believers.

"[God] did not discriminate between us and them. . . . We believe it is through the grace of our Lord Jesus that we are saved, just as they are."

ACTS 15:9, 11

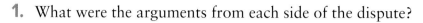

Know It

1. What were the arguments from each side of the dispute?

2. What might have motivated the players in this debate?

3. Look again at the council's resolution in Acts 15:19–29. How would the different groups of people involved in this dispute need to act differently going forward?

Explore It

The Dispute

As we have already seen in Acts, Paul faced considerable opposition from the unbelieving Jews early in his ministry. However, the next phase of Paul's ministry would introduce a new twist: opposition from Christian Jews.

Near the end of Paul's first missionary journey, a group known as the Judaizers heavily infiltrated the churches that Paul had just established in the province of Galatia and they started to change church doctrine. These Judaizers were professed Christians who nonetheless insisted that other Christians follow the laws of Judaism. They insisted that circumcision and observance of Mosaic Law were essential for salvation. They tried to impose their regulations on Gentile converts as well as Jewish ones.

The Judaizers' doctrine contradicted everything Paul had been preaching to the Galatians about their newfound freedom in Christ. It suggested that Christ's sacrifice on the cross was not enough—and Paul wanted nothing to do with such a suggestion! He wrote the very first of his letters in the Bible to the Galatians, making his case clear: "We . . . know that a person is not justified by the works of the law, but by faith in Jesus Christ" (Galatians 2:15–16).

This letter to the Galatians shows Paul at his angriest. He had just finished planting these young churches and establishing leadership there, only to see others try to corrupt and destroy these churches. He wrote:

> I am astonished that you are so quickly deserting the one who called you to live in the grace of Christ and are turning to a different gospel—which is really no gospel at all. Evidently some people are throwing you into confusion and are trying to pervert the gospel of Christ. But even if we or an angel

from heaven should preach a gospel other than the one we preached to you, let them be under God's curse! (1:6–8).

In fact, to emphasize the passion of his message, Paul actually took the pen from his scribe and wrote the end of the letter himself, in large letters (6:11)!

The Council

Paul and Barnabas were appointed to go to Jerusalem to meet with the apostles and elders to resolve this issue. This meeting has come to be known as the Jerusalem Council. Peter and James were leaders of the church in Jerusalem, made up predominantly of Jewish Christians. However, Peter had also personally taken part in bringing the gospel to the Gentiles (Acts 10) and thus understood the issue from both sides.

The important matter at this point was to uphold the freedom from sin and the salvation that Christ had provided, while, at the same time, maintaining unity within the church. After much

The Apostle Paul

discussion, Peter declared about the Judaizers, "Why do you try to test God by putting on the necks of Gentiles a yoke that neither we nor our ancestors have been able to bear?" (15:10). The council had come to a decision.

The Resolution

The resolution, first declared by James, was "that we should not make it difficult for the Gentiles who are turning to God. Instead we should write to them, telling them to abstain from food polluted by idols, from sexual immorality, from the meat of strangled animals and from blood" (15:19–20). James's warning to abstain from sexual immorality seems clear enough today, but in fact, all four prohibitions can be tied back to the first item: idolatry. Worship of other gods in ancient times often involved the eating of blood as well as temple prostitution, and Roman times were certainly no exception. It is also worth noting that the commandment to abstain from "what has been strangled, and from blood" actually predates Mosaic Law—going back to God's covenant with Noah after the flood (Genesis 9:4).

Freedom in Christ

The bottom line, for Jewish and Gentile believers alike, was that *freedom* in Christ meant *living* in Christ, and that meant avoiding all things and behaviors that honored other gods, for that would have dishonored the one true God. Paul would make this same point years later, in his letter to the Romans:

> What then? Shall we sin because we are not under the law but under grace? By no means! . . . But thanks be to God that, though you used to be slaves to sin, you have come to obey from your heart the pattern of teaching that has now claimed your allegiance. You have been set free from sin and have become slaves to righteousness (6:15–18).

Though the council helped make clear for believers what freedom and living in Christ really meant, the Judaizers would continue to oppose Paul's mission. More than a decade later, Paul would warn the church at Philippi about the Judaizers:

> Watch out for those dogs, those evildoers, those mutilators of the flesh. For it is we who are the circumcision, we who serve God by his Spirit, who boast in Christ Jesus, and who put no confidence in the flesh (Philippians 3:2–3).

Live It

Paul and the apostles confronted a situation that threatened to tear the early church apart. Jesus had come to set his people free, and the Judaizers had come to re-imprison them. Thankfully, Paul and the other apostles resolved the situation in a way that reflected Jesus Christ, that held true to the gospel message, and that strengthened the early church. As a result, the church was "glad for its encouraging message" (Acts 15:31).

Even today, we wrestle with how to live out our freedom in Christ and at the same time honor God with our actions. Like Paul's confrontation with the Judaizers, sometimes we will need to confront similar false teachings in our churches today. But sometimes we're the ones who need to be confronted! The important thing, now as then, is to love others even as we maintain the truth of the gospel of Christ.

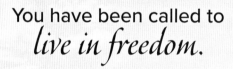

You have been called to
live in freedom.
But don't use your freedom to
satisfy your sinful nature.

Instead, use your freedom to
serve one another in love.

GALATIANS 5:13 NLT

Life Application Questions

1. As seen in his letter to the Galatians, Paul was adamant that the gospel not be perverted in any way. What are some ways you've seen people try to corrupt the gospel?

2. When has God led you to rethink your own personal "laws" about what it means to live like a Christian? What has changed in your life and relationships as a result of the rethinking?

3. How have you experienced freedom in Christ? What has Christ freed you from?

4. Suppose someone joined your church who genuinely appeared to believe in Jesus, but had very strict opinions about what following Christ should look like for other believers. What would you do?

5. Suppose someone joined your church who genuinely appeared to believe in Jesus, but acted and worshiped in ways that seemed not to honor God. What would you do? And also, what attitudes might you need to check in yourself before doing so (see Matthew 7:3–5)?

6. After reflecting on the early Christians' "sharp dispute," what is one takeaway you've learned about dealing with disputes among believers?

Prayer

Lord, we thank you for the freedom you've given us. We also know that freedom comes with responsibility. We want to be free of conflict and to be faithful to you, but sometimes we can't do both. Help us to know when and how to speak both your truth and your love to others—and help us to be willing to admit we're wrong when we need to. Give us the wisdom to know how to best live out the freedom you've given us, that your love might be shared and made known to the world. In Jesus' name, amen.

This Coming Week

Consider the following options for living out your faith in response to this session's study—or come up with one of your own. Then, *do it.*

- Think again about someone you identified (or at least thought of) while working through this session. How might you talk with that person, not necessarily to confront that person, but to share a perspective that he or she needs to hear about what it really means to have freedom in Christ? Find the time, summon your courage, and make it happen.

- Grab a piece of paper or an index card. On one side, complete the following sentence:
  "One lie that I find easy to believe is _____."
  On the other side, complete this sentence:
  "One truth I find hard to believe is _____."
  Pray to stay committed to God's truth so that you'll be able to not only distinguish the truth from the lies in your life but also counter those lies with the truth.

PAUL'S DISRUPTIVE MESSAGE

The Power of the Gospel

ACTS 19:1–41

Paul's Disruptive Message

An encounter with Jesus Christ changes everything. Paul understood this firsthand. It was this good news, the gospel of Jesus, that Paul had been called to boldly proclaim.

Think about the gospel message: a humble Savior crucified like a common criminal but raised from the dead in glory; he calls *all* people to trust in him for forgiveness of their sins and to begin living new lives of radical grace, mercy, and obedience to the one true God. This kind of gospel message wouldn't just challenge the status quo of an ungodly world, it would throw it into turmoil.

In this session, we'll focus on Paul's ministry in the city of Ephesus where he had spent more time than any other place on his missionary journeys. The story of what happened in Ephesus is the story of how powerfully and wonderfully disruptive is the gospel of Jesus!

Read It

Key Bible Passage

For this session, read Acts 19:1–41.

Optional Reading

Acts 15:36–20:12

This extra reading covers from the time immediately following the Jerusalem Council to partway through Paul's third missionary journey. (It also includes the *Key Bible Passage* for this session.)

"A number who had practiced sorcery brought their scrolls together and burned them publicly. . . . In this way the word of the Lord spread widely and grew in power."

ACTS 19:19–20

Know It

1. What was Paul's approach to proclaiming the gospel message in the city of Ephesus? What did he do and where did he go?

2. Why do you think the sons of Sceva were unable to cast out a demon, even using Jesus' name?

3. Why were many of the Ephesians so passionate about protecting the worship of Artemis? What would you have thought if you were one of the city's silversmiths?

The City of Ephesus

Ephesus was one of the largest cities in the Roman Empire. Its temple for the goddess of fertility, Artemis (Diana)—about 425 feet long, 200 feet wide, 60 feet high, and supported by 127 columns—was one of the seven wonders of the ancient world. This harbor city had a booming tourist industry, with craftsmen creating souvenirs of Artemis for visitors to take home with them. Ephesus was a pilgrimage site, as well as a major banking center in Asia Minor. It was also known to be a city steeped in superstition and occult practices.

By the time Paul first arrived at Ephesus, the city was already more dependent on the religious tourist trade than on harbor traffic, as the harbor had begun filling with silt.

©Serg Zastavkin/Shutterstock.com

Model of the Temple of Artemis

The Gospel in Ephesus

After some time in Antioch, Paul set out on his third missionary journey, first revisiting the churches of Galatia and Phrygia and then Ephesus. Paul remained in Ephesus for two years, preaching the gospel initially in the synagogues and then in the public lecture halls. God did great miracles through Paul in Ephesus "so that even handkerchiefs and aprons that had touched him were taken to the sick, and their illnesses were cured and the evil spirits left them" (Acts 19:12). These handkerchiefs and aprons were likely used by Ephesian craftsmen who had come to believe in Christ.

Because of this explosion of the miraculous, some wandering Jewish exorcists claiming to be able to cast out evil spirits saw a business opportunity. Among them were the seven sons of the so-called "high priest" Sceva who now tried to change their business model by casting out evil spirits in Jesus' name. In using the name of Jesus like a magic word, they failed miserably against a demon. They were, in fact, overpowered by the evil spirit, and

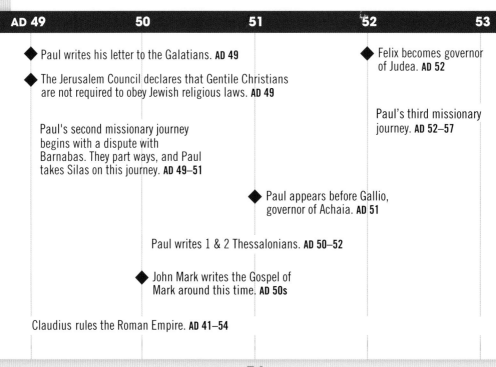

AD 49   50   51   52   53

Paul writes his letter to the Galatians. **AD 49**

The Jerusalem Council declares that Gentile Christians are not required to obey Jewish religious laws. **AD 49**

Paul's second missionary journey begins with a dispute with Barnabas. They part ways, and Paul takes Silas on this journey. **AD 49–51**

Felix becomes governor of Judea. **AD 52**

Paul's third missionary journey. **AD 52–57**

Paul appears before Gallio, governor of Achaia. **AD 51**

Paul writes 1 & 2 Thessalonians. **AD 50–52**

John Mark writes the Gospel of Mark around this time. **AD 50s**

Claudius rules the Roman Empire. **AD 41–54**

they "ran out of that house naked and bleeding" (19:16). But God has a way of taking human attempts at perverting the gospel and making them a catalyst for spreading the real gospel even further. News of this episode shocked the Ephesians. Many "who had practiced magic arts brought their books together and burned them in the sight of all. And they counted the value of them and found it came to fifty thousand pieces of silver" (19:19 ESV). These scrolls were probably made of papyrus or parchment, so their high value likely had nothing to do with the quality of their construction but with their supposed magical content. Salvation in Christ was far more valuable to these new Ephesian converts than their "magic" scrolls.

This proved to be a serious problem to the city's silversmiths who were dependent on the religious tourist trade generated by the temple of Artemis. The power of the gospel not only was changing the religious identity of Ephesus, but it also was bad for business. A riot ensued. It became clear that it was time for Paul to leave the city in which he had invested so much time.

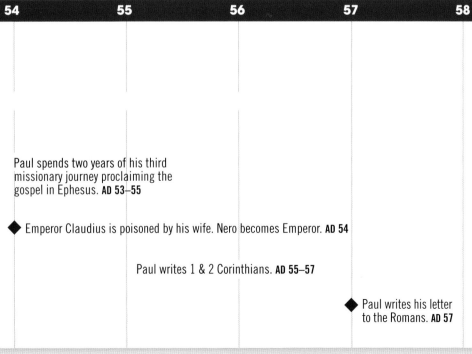

| 54 | 55 | 56 | 57 | 58 |

Paul spends two years of his third missionary journey proclaiming the gospel in Ephesus. **AD 53–55**

◆ Emperor Claudius is poisoned by his wife. Nero becomes Emperor. **AD 54**

Paul writes 1 & 2 Corinthians. **AD 55–57**

◆ Paul writes his letter to the Romans. **AD 57**

Travelers: Paul, Silas, Timothy, Luke, Priscilla and Aquila

Main Route: Syria, Asia Minor, Greece, Judea (2,800 mi; 4,506 km)

1. **Antioch of Syria:** Paul and Barnabas disagree about who should go with them. Barnabas takes John Mark with him to Cyprus. Paul takes Silas.

2. **Cilicia:** Paul and Silas deliver a letter from the Jerusalem church.

3. **Derbe, Lystra, Iconium:** Timothy joins them. (Timothy would become Paul's protégé and play a large role in the early church.)

4. **Troas:** Paul has a vision of a man from Macedonia calling him to come help people there, so Paul and his team head further westward, into Macedonia.

5. **Samothrace, Neapolis, Philippi:** Lydia, a wealthy businesswoman, is converted in the Macedonian city of Philippi. When a fortune-telling slave girl is converted, her owners start a riot, and Paul and Silas are thrown in jail. After an earthquake, Paul and Silas stay in their cells. The jailer is converted.

6. **Amphipolis, Apollonia, Thessalonica:** A mob in Thessalonica tries to have Paul and Silas arrested.

7. **Berea:** The people in the synagogue receive the message eagerly. Silas and Timothy stay here while Paul goes on.

8. **Athens (Mars Hill/Areopagus):** Paul sees an altar to an unknown god and preaches to the thinkers of Athens.

9. **Corinth:** Silas and Timothy rejoin Paul. He meets Aquila and Priscilla, who also join him. During Paul's year-and-a-half stay here, he writes to believers in Thessalonica.

10. **Cenchreae:** Paul gets his hair cut because he had taken a vow. No more details are given.

11. **Ephesus:** Paul establishes a local church in this city, leaving Priscilla and Aquila here to tend to it.

12. **Caesarea, Jerusalem, Antioch of Syria:** Paul returns to his home base of Antioch by way of Jerusalem.

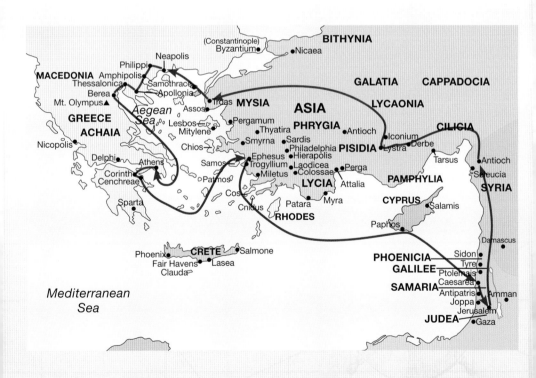

PAUL'S THIRD MISSIONARY JOURNEY
AD 52–57; Acts 18:23–21:16

Travelers: Paul, Timothy, Luke, others

Main Route: Asia Minor, Greece, Phoenicia (2,700 mi; 4,345 km)

1. **Antioch of Syria, Galatia, Phrygia:** Paul visits the churches in this area again.

2. **Ephesus:** Paul stays here two years. So many people convert that the silversmiths who manufacture idols start a riot.

3. **Macedonia, Greece (Achaia):** Paul gives encouraging words to believers in this region. He stays three months.

4. **Philippi, Troas:** In Troas while Paul is preaching, a young man falls asleep, falls from a third-story window, and dies. Paul revives him.

5. **Assos, Mitylene, Samos, Miletus:** Elders from Ephesus meet the ship at Miletus and Paul tells them he expects to be imprisoned in Jerusalem.

6. **Cos, Rhodes, Patara, Tyre:** In Tyre, disciples warn Paul not to go to Jerusalem.

7. **Ptolemais, Caesarea:** In Caesarea, a prophet predicts that Paul will be imprisoned and handed over to the Gentiles.

8. **Jerusalem:** The missionaries report to the church leaders, who urge Paul to participate in a purification ritual at the temple to counteract rumors that Christianity is anti-Jewish.

BITHYNIA
(Constantinople)
Byzantium
Nicaea

Neapolis
Philippi
MACEDONIA Amphipolis
Thessalonica
Berea
Mt. Olympus
Samothrace
Apollonia
Assos
Troas
MYSIA
Pergamum
Thyatira
Smyrna
Sardis
Philadelphia
Hierapolis
Laodicea
Colossae

GALATIA
CAPPADOCIA
LYCAONIA
Antioch
Iconium
Lystra
Derbe
CILICIA
Tarsus
Antioch
Seleucia
SYRIA

GREECE
ACHAIA
Nicopolis
Aegean
Sea
Lesbos
Mitylene
Chios
Samos
Trogyllium
Miletus
ASIA
PHRYGIA
PISIDIA

Delphi
Athens
Corinth
Cenchreae
Sparta
Patmos
Cos
Cnidus
Ephesus

LYCIA
Perga
Attalia
PAMPHYLIA

Patara
Myra
RHODES
CYPRUS
Salamis
Paphos

Mediterranean
Sea

Phoenix
CRETE
Salmone
Fair Havens
Lasea
Clauda

PHOENICIA
GALILEE
Sidon
Tyre
Ptolemais
Caesarea
SAMARIA
Antipatris
Amman
Joppa
Jerusalem
JUDEA
Gaza
Damascus

Acropolis of Lindos and the bay of St. Paul, Rhodes

Paul planted the church at Ephesus and spent more than two years ministering to the people there. The power of the good news of Jesus moved dramatically in the lives of the Ephesians, which in turn brought opposition to these changes. Despite (and even through) this persecution, the church at Ephesus flourished.

Investing in others—and in the community around us—for the long haul isn't easy. As it was with Paul in Ephesus, some people will embrace the good news, others will twist what we do and say (both intentionally and unintentionally), and the gospel message might anger some people. But lives will be changed. People will be healed. And through us, the people around us will see the power and love of Christ Jesus.

Paul preaching in Ephesus as sorcerers burn their scrolls (Acts 19).

Life Application Questions

1. Like the sons of Sceva who tried to use the name of Jesus for their own gain, what's an example from today's society of people using the gospel or Jesus himself for selfish ends?

2. What is it about the gospel message that makes it so disruptive to the world's status quo? Give an example or two.

3. Have you experienced the disruptive power of the gospel in your own life? If so, what happened?

4. Think about a time when you've invested resources and energy in another person or ministry. What was most rewarding about that time? What "miracles" took place?

5. What are some obstacles or fears you face in investing time and energy into others?

6. Who or what is God calling you to invest more in right now? What changes will you need to make in other parts of your life to make that time available?

Prayer

Lord, you've given us so many good things: relationships, accomplishments, opportunities to serve. But just because they're good things doesn't mean they're easy things. Help us to see past the difficulties to see what you see: the people you love and the lives you want to change. Help us to know where to invest our lives in others. Help us to be people willing to change so that you can use us to bring the power of the gospel to the world around us. In Jesus' name, amen.

This Coming Week

Consider the following options for living out your faith in response to this session's study—or come up with one of your own. Then, *do it.*

- In whom do you need to invest more time? How does God want to use you to help that person see Jesus more clearly? Where do you need to see Jesus more clearly, as you reach out? Confess any fears you have up front, ask God to give you the wisdom and compassion you need, and then follow his leading now.

- Jesus calls us in no uncertain terms to reach out to those in need: the homeless, the stranger, the hungry, and the incarcerated (Matthew 25:31–46). Organize a group visit to a soup kitchen, homeless shelter, crisis pregnancy center, or the local jail. Maybe organize a fun social outing for families in need. Think also about how you can make this a regular practice, rather than just a one-time event.

Notes

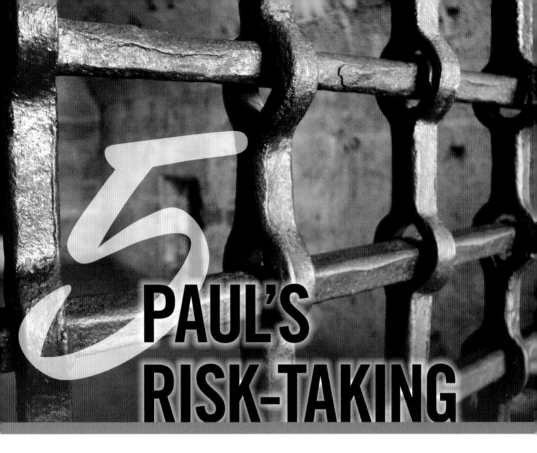

5
PAUL'S
RISK-TAKING

Arrest, Trials, and Prison

ACTS 20:17–24
ACTS 21:17–22:29

Paul's Risk-Taking

Doing the right thing can be the hardest thing to do—especially when all of your well-meaning friends are telling you not to do it.

This is the situation Paul faced as he resolved to go to Jerusalem. With a farewell address to the elders of the church in Ephesus, Paul headed toward Jerusalem, "not knowing what [would] happen to [him] there" (Acts 20:22). Nevertheless, the Holy Spirit had compelled him to go. How could he deny the Spirit's leading? He didn't.

In fact, most of the things Paul's friends predicted and feared came true in Jerusalem. Yet, in the end, it all turned out to be for God's glory because it was all by God's leading.

Read It

Key Bible Passage

For this session, read Acts 20:17–24; 21:17–22:29.

Optional Reading

Acts 20:13–24:27

This extra reading covers from Paul's farewell to the Ephesian elders through his imprisonment in Caesarea. (It also includes the *Key Bible Passage* for this session.)

"I consider my life worth nothing to me; my only aim is to finish the race and complete the task the Lord Jesus has given me—the task of testifying to the good news of God's grace."

ACTS 20:24

Know It

1. According to Paul, *why* did he have to go to Jerusalem (20:17–24)?

2. Imagine being Paul as the events in Jerusalem unfold (21:17–36). Everything the Spirit and the disciples predicted is starting to come to pass, right before your eyes. How would you respond? Would you be afraid, emboldened, something else?

3. What were the responses to Paul's message (21:37–22:29)? What's your response to Paul's message, especially as you've spent the last several weeks looking at his life story? What jumps out at you as you "heard" Paul tell his own story?

Warnings on the Way to Jerusalem

Shortly after the riot in Ephesus, "Paul sent for the disciples and, after encouraging them, said goodbye and set out for Macedonia" (Acts 20:1)—a trip he had already intended to make (19:21–22). Paul revisited several churches in Macedonia and Greece, before returning to Troas in Asia Minor. At this point, Paul made a momentous decision: He indeed would return to Jerusalem, knowing he would likely be arrested there.

On his journey to Jerusalem, he met with the elders from Ephesus—the church where he had invested so much—and gave what he was convinced would be his last farewell to them. Paul and the Ephesians had been through a lot together—and the tearful goodbye in Acts 20:37–38 illustrates just how much. Nonetheless, despite all the good things accomplished in Ephesus, Paul had an even stronger calling upon him. He was determined to "finish the race and complete the task the Lord Jesus [had] given [him]" (20:24).

The Ephesian elders didn't want Paul to go to Jerusalem—and they weren't alone. As Paul completed his third missionary journey— and much like Jesus prior to his death as he "resolutely set out for Jerusalem" (Luke 9:51)—Paul was repeatedly warned by prophets and other disciples of what awaited him.

While in Tyre on his way to Jerusalem, Paul and his entourage (including Luke, the author of the book of Acts) sought out the disciples there and stayed for seven days. "Through the Spirit [the disciples] urged Paul not to go to Jerusalem" (Acts 21:4).

This brings up an interesting question: Was Paul disobeying the Spirit by continuing to Jerusalem? The short answer is no. As you may recall from Acts 20, the Spirit had already told Paul to go to Jerusalem: "Compelled by the Spirit, I am going to Jerusalem, not knowing what will happen to me there. I only know that in every city the Holy Spirit warns me that prison and hardships are facing me" (20:22–23). Though Paul didn't know exactly what would happen to him in Jerusalem, he understood that captivity and persecution were awaiting him. It is likely that when the Spirit had confirmed this to the disciples, they had responded much as Peter first did when Jesus had first told his disciples that he was headed to Jerusalem to be killed (Matthew 16:21–23). Their response was out of fear and concern for their leader rather than out of faith in God's sovereignty in the matter.

In Caesarea, Paul stayed with Philip, "one of the Seven" who had, years before, been chosen to oversee a food distribution ministry in Jerusalem (Acts 6:1–6; 21:8). It's worth remembering that Stephen, whose stoning Paul had once approved of, was also one of the seven (8:1). Thus, it is clear that Philip had forgiven Paul for his role in Stephen's murder.

Also at Caesarea, the prophet Agabus predicted Paul's arrest and imprisonment, and again, the disciples—including Luke, it would appear—begged Paul not to continue. But Paul answered:

> "Why are you weeping and breaking my heart? I am ready not only to be bound, but also to die in Jerusalem for the name of the Lord Jesus." When he would not be dissuaded, we gave up and said, "The Lord's will be done" (21:13–14).

Paul was far less concerned about the dangers and suffering he would face and far more concerned with following Jesus, no matter what the cost. We can see this single-minded attitude throughout Paul's writings on his way to Jerusalem (2 Corinthians 4:17–18; 6:3–10).

In Jerusalem

Upon arriving in Jerusalem, Paul was welcomed by the brothers and then by James and the elders (Acts 21:17–18). About eight years had passed since Paul's visit to Jerusalem when the Jerusalem Council was held. In that time, God had used Paul greatly among the Gentiles, and when Paul shared with the church at Jerusalem about all that God had done, "they praised God" (21:20).

A curious question arises about the incident in Acts 21:20–26. Why did Paul, who had been preaching freedom in Christ across the known world, choose to go through the Jewish religious rites of purification?

It's worth noting that this wasn't the first time Paul had done (or requested) something like this. We saw that at Cenchreae Paul had cut his hair because he was under a vow (18:18)—generally believed to be the vow of a Nazarite, a voluntary vow of separation to the Lord (Numbers 6:1–21). Even more radically,

Ancient mikvah, a bath used for the purpose of ritual immersion in Judaism

Paul had the Gentile Timothy circumcised shortly after the Jerusalem Council, "because of the Jews who lived in that area, for they all knew that [Timothy's] father was a Greek" (Acts 16:3).

On the surface, these incidents seem out of line with what Paul taught. However, they line up perfectly with his *bigger* mission. Especially as a Jew, Paul would not have wanted to go out of his way to offend his fellow Jews, even as he clearly preached to them that such rites were in no way necessary for salvation. The clearest rationale for these actions can be seen in Paul's first letter to the Corinthians, written shortly before his arrival in Jerusalem:

> Though I am free and belong to no one, I have made myself a slave to everyone, to win as many as possible. To the Jews I became like a Jew, to win the Jews. To those under the law I became like one under the law (though I myself am not under the law), so as to win those under the law. . . . I do all this for the sake of the gospel, that I may share in its blessings (1 Corinthians 9:19–23).

Paul's Arrest

Near the end of his voluntary purification, Paul again entered the temple at Jerusalem. Upon seeing Paul, "Jews from Asia . . . stirred up the whole crowd and laid hands on him" and accused him of bringing Trophimus the Ephesian, one of his traveling companions, into the temple with him (Acts 21:27–29). Such an accusation flew in the face of the purification Paul had been willing to undergo for the sake of his fellow Jews, but clearly the crowd was willing to believe this slander against Paul.

Paul was dragged out of the temple. The mob beat him, until the Roman army arrived and put Paul in chains. Paul had to be physically carried away by the soldiers "because of the violence of the mob" (21:35). Before he was brought into the barracks, however, he asked to speak to the crowd. It was no small miracle in itself that at this point "there was a great hush" (21:40 ESV).

Standing before his own persecutors, Paul shared his story. He too had once been a persecutor of Christians in Jerusalem before his encounter with Christ. He even mentioned his own role in the death of Stephen, before making a statement (just like Stephen had) that pushed the hostile audience over the edge: "The Lord said to me, 'Go; I will send you far away to the Gentiles'" (22:21).

At this, they began "shouting and throwing off their cloaks and flinging dust into the air, [so] the commander ordered that Paul be taken into the barracks. He directed that he be flogged and interrogated" (22:23–24). Instead, Paul declared his Roman citizenship to the centurion and asked, "Is it legal for you to flog a Roman citizen who hasn't even been found guilty?" (22:25). The answer was obviously *no*. His interrogators stopped.

Yet the hardships Paul faced didn't stop. Paul stood trial before the Jewish court—the Sanhedrin—and then Felix the governor of Judea. But Paul's message about "righteousness, self-control and the judgment to come" (24:25) made Felix afraid, so he had Paul sent to prison, where Paul remained for two years.

Soreg Inscription. First-century warning in Greek to Gentiles to avoid areas of the temple that were off limits under penalty of death. It reads, "No foreigner shall enter within the balustrade of the temple and whoever shall be caught shall be responsible for his own death that will follow in consequence [of] his trespassing."

Parallels between Jesus' and Paul's Final Entries into Jerusalem

JESUS	PAUL
Jesus determined to go to Jerusalem, despite the dangers he knew awaited him (Luke 9:51; 13:33).	Paul was compelled by the Spirit to go to Jerusalem, despite the dangers he knew awaited him (Acts 19:21; 20:22–23; 21:8–14).
Jesus arrived in Jerusalem, was welcomed by large crowds, and went to the temple soon afterward (Luke 19:28–48).	Paul arrived in Jerusalem, was welcomed by the disciples there, and went to the temple soon afterward (Acts 21:17–26).
Jesus was arrested by a Jewish mob, then turned over to the Roman governor for trial (Luke 22:47-54; 23:1–25).	Paul was seized by a Jewish mob that wanted him killed, and later stood trial before Roman governors (Acts 21:30–36; 23:23–26:32).
During questioning, one of the high priest's officers struck Jesus in the face (John 18:22–23).	The high priest ordered those nearby to strike Paul on the mouth (Acts 23:2–5).
Jesus was questioned by Sadducees, who did not believe in the resurrection (Luke 20:27–38).	Paul pitted the Pharisees against the Sadducees regarding the resurrection (Acts 23:6–9).
At the Last Supper, Jesus took bread, blessed it, broke it, and gave it to the disciples to eat (Matthew 26:26–28; Luke 22:15–20).	On his way to Rome, Paul took bread, gave thanks, broke it, and ate it (Acts 27:35).

Live It

Despite the warnings he had received, Paul entered Jerusalem and spoke boldly, considering his life less important than the Savior he was sent to preach about. He faced pressure from others and his own fears responsibly and chose to focus on Jesus instead.

Paul had taken a risk and followed the Holy Spirit's leading. With Paul ending up in prison, to some it may have looked like the risk didn't pay off. Yet Paul knew that obeying God's calling upon his life was above everything else, no matter what his present circumstances looked like. As Paul wrote in his letter to the Romans, "We know that in all things God works for the good of those who love him, who have been called according to his purpose" (8:28).

We have the same opportunity to choose Jesus and follow wherever he leads—even when he leads us into uncomfortable and dangerous places. Like Paul, we will receive the wisdom and strength we need *when* we need it, because we follow the One who is the source of all wisdom and strength.

Life Application Questions

1. Think of a spiritual risk-taker you know. What stands out about that person?

2. When has God urged you to take a risk? Did you hear a warning that made you want to turn back? How did you respond?

3. Even though it was no longer required of him, Paul was willing to purify himself to make his testimony acceptable to the Jews. What barriers that don't have to be there might stand between you and those you want to share Christ with? How can you move past those barriers while still staying true to Christ?

4. You may not have been in front of a big crowd like Paul, but when have you spoken up for Christ or shared your testimony? How did people respond?

5. What's your "Jerusalem" right now? In other words, where is God calling you to take a step (or leap) of faith?

6. What warnings or fears do you need to set aside in order to take that step of faith? At the same time, is there any wisdom in those warnings that could help you as you move forward?

Prayer

God, we know that your way is better than our ways, yet sometimes we try to avoid that way because we think it's too difficult. Give us courage in our uncertainty. Give us peace as we face opposition and trials. We want to honor you with our choices, not to shy away from the responsibility of following you. You have authority in our lives, and we trust you to lead us—and to protect us where you're leading us. In Jesus' name, amen.

This Coming Week

Hard things don't have to be big things. Sometimes the way to move forward is to deal with our attitudes or actions. Target one area this week and take a step in the right direction. Connect with someone you've judged or had a disagreement with and set things right. Fulfill a commitment you made to God, yourself, or others that you haven't kept. Whatever you decide, ask a friend, a roommate, or family member to keep you accountable.

Notes

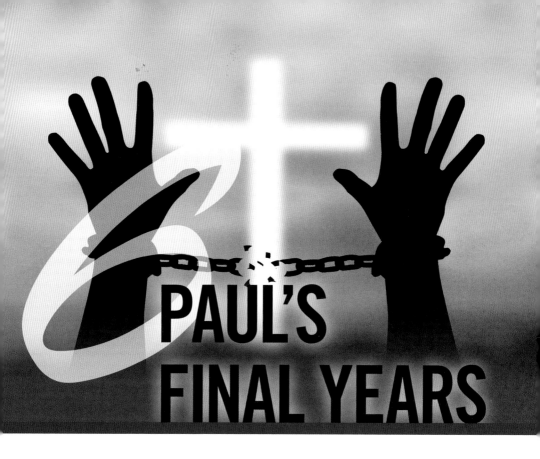

PAUL'S FINAL YEARS

In Chains for Christ

ACTS 28:16–31
PHILIPPIANS 1:12–26

Shortly after Paul's arrest in Jerusalem, the Lord appeared to him and said, "Take courage! As you have testified about me in Jerusalem, so you must also testify in Rome" (Acts 23:11). Waiting in prison in Caesarea for two years, Paul knew that his story would not end there—he would go to Rome.

When the new governor of Judea, Festus, arrived in Caesarea, Paul did something surprising: he appealed his case to Caesar. To which Festus replied, "To Caesar you will go!" (25:12). This began Paul's long journey to Rome.

Paul did eventually arrive in Rome as he had desired and as the Lord had revealed to him. But he arrived in chains! He remained for two years in Rome under guarded house arrest.

How should trials and hardships be viewed—simply as things to escape from or as opportunities to learn what God wants to teach through them? Paul chose the latter. While he spent much of the last decade of his life under house arrest or in prison, Paul didn't bemoan his fate. Rather, no matter where he was, he found opportunities to share the gospel and encourage believers who were carrying out the work he had helped start.

Read It

Key Bible Passage

For this session, read Acts 28:16–31 and Philippians 1:12–26.

Optional Reading

Acts 25:1–28:31

This extra reading covers from Paul's journey to Rome through the end of the book of Acts. (It includes the *Key Bible Passage* from Acts, but be sure to also read the passage from Philippians.)

"What has happened to me has actually served to advance the gospel. As a result, it has become clear throughout the whole palace guard and to everyone else that I am in chains for Christ."

PHILIPPIANS 1:12–13

Know It

1. Though Paul faced many restrictions under house arrest in Rome, what was he still able to do (Acts 28:16–31)?

2. According to Paul in Philippians 1:12–26, how did he view his hardships? What good came out of them, both for him and for others around him?

3. As you read about Paul in these Bible passages, what was your reaction to his attitude and actions? (Check any that apply.)

   ❏ Hard to believe

   ❏ Encouraging

   ❏ Unrealistic

   ❏ Something I want to strive for

   ❏ Other: _____

The Kingdom of God in Rome

Paul wasn't the first Christian to set foot in Rome. We don't know who first brought the gospel to Rome, but we know there was already a church in Rome when Paul wrote his epistle to the Romans in AD 57, just before he was arrested in Jerusalem. Rome was the epicenter of the most powerful empire in Paul's time. Believers in Rome faced many challenges to their faith. A powerful, rich, and influential city like Rome harbored many different religious practices that contradicted the Christian faith. In this letter, Paul told the Roman Christians, "I long to see you so that I may impart to you some spiritual gift to make you strong" (Romans 1:11).

Luke, the writer of Acts, tells his readers that in Rome, Paul "proclaimed the kingdom of God and taught about the Lord Jesus Christ—with all boldness and without hindrance!" (Acts 28:31). Here in the most powerful kingdom of the earth, Paul boldly declared the kingdom of God.

While under house arrest in Rome, Paul wrote several epistles in the New Testament, including the letter to the church in Philippi. In this letter, he refers to his struggles several times, but he also looks past those struggles and rejoices that even his confinement resulted in good. As he wrote, "It has become clear throughout the whole palace guard and to everyone else that I am in chains for Christ" (Philippians 1:13). The implication is that some of the guard (and people in the palace) responded to some degree to the gospel message. However, Paul's influence clearly extended outside the confines of prison, as his closing comments in this letter indicate: "All God's people here send you greetings, *especially those who belong to Caesar's household"* (4:22, emphasis added). Recall what God had told Ananias about Paul after Paul's conversion on the road to Damascus: "This man [Paul] is my chosen instrument to proclaim my name to the Gentiles and their kings and to the people of Israel" (Acts 9:15). In the final chapter of Acts, we see Paul doing exactly that.

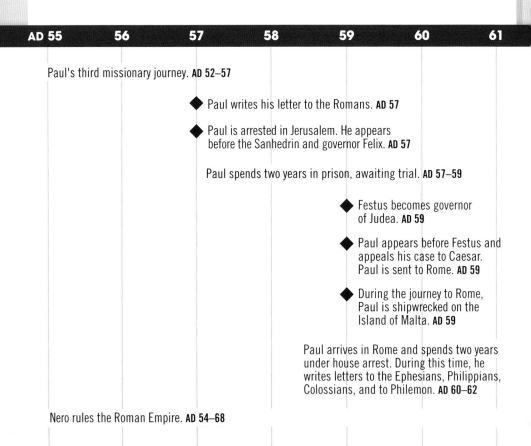

| AD 55 | 56 | 57 | 58 | 59 | 60 | 61 |

Paul's third missionary journey. **AD 52–57**

◆ Paul writes his letter to the Romans. **AD 57**

◆ Paul is arrested in Jerusalem. He appears before the Sanhedrin and governor Felix. **AD 57**

Paul spends two years in prison, awaiting trial. **AD 57–59**

◆ Festus becomes governor of Judea. **AD 59**

◆ Paul appears before Festus and appeals his case to Caesar. Paul is sent to Rome. **AD 59**

◆ During the journey to Rome, Paul is shipwrecked on the Island of Malta. **AD 59**

Paul arrives in Rome and spends two years under house arrest. During this time, he writes letters to the Ephesians, Philippians, Colossians, and to Philemon. **AD 60–62**

Nero rules the Roman Empire. **AD 54–68**

The Forum Romanum in Rome

62	63	64	65	66	67	68

◆ James the brother of Jesus is martyred. **AD 62**

◆ Luke finishes writing his Gospel and the book of Acts. **AD 62**

Paul is released from house arrest in Rome and travels throughout the Mediterranean. **AD 62–64**

◆ Paul writes his first letter to Timothy around this time. **AD 62–66**

◆ Peter writes his letters (1 & 2 Peter) around this time. **AD 64–65**

◆ Paul writes his letter to Titus around this time. **AD 64–66**

◆ A fire breaks out in Rome. Nero blames the Christians. **AD 64**

Nero persecutes Christians in Rome. **AD 64–68**

◆ Paul is imprisoned in Rome around this time. **AD 64**

◆ Paul writes his second letter to Timothy around this time. **AD 66–67**

Paul and Peter are martyred in Rome. **AD 66–68**

PAUL'S ARREST AND JOURNEY TO ROME
AD 57–62; Acts 21:17–28:31

Travelers: Paul, Roman guards, Luke, others

Main Route: Judea, Asia Minor, Crete, Malta, Sicily, Italy (2,250 mi; 3,621 km)

1. **Jerusalem:** After arresting Paul, the Roman commander learns of a death threat against Paul, so he orders an armed escort to take Paul to Caesarea.

2. **Antipatris, Caesarea:** Paul is tried before Felix, the governor of Judea, but Felix leaves Paul in prison for two years. Paul again stands trial, but this time before Festus, the new governor. Paul demands his right as a Roman citizen and appeals his case to Caesar. King Agrippa II visits Festus, and Paul appears before him as well. It's decided that Paul should go to Rome.

3. **Sidon:** The centurion in charge of Paul lets him visit with friends here. Then Paul boards a ship and sets sail for Rome.

4. **Myra, Fair Havens:** Paul recommends that the ship stay in safe harbor, but the centurion orders the ship to sail on.

5. **Malta:** After a two-week storm, the ship is wrecked near the island of Malta. Everyone on the ship makes it to shore after the shipwreck. While putting wood on a campfire, Paul is bitten by a venomous snake, but it does not harm him.

6. **Syracuse, Rhegium, Puteoli:** In Puteoli, Paul stays with believers for a week.

7. **Appii Forum, Three Taverns:** Paul is met by Christians from Rome.

8. **Rome:** Paul remains under house arrest for two years, where he writes Ephesians, Colossians, Philemon, and Philippians.

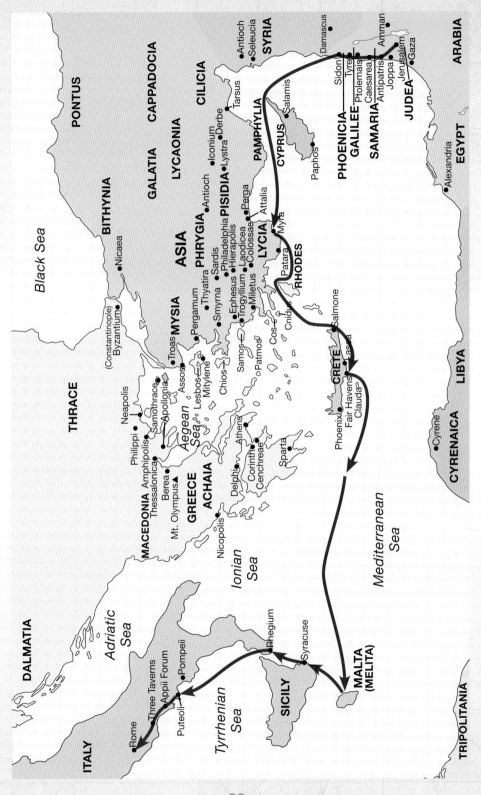

After Acts

There is considerable debate about the final years of Paul's life after the close of the book of Acts. The most-accepted theory is that after two years of house arrest, Paul was released and allowed to travel again. During this fourth missionary journey, Paul traveled throughout the Mediterranean:

- Macedonia (1 Timothy 1:3)

- Troas (2 Timothy 4:13)

- Miletus (2 Timothy 4:20)

- Crete (Titus 1:5)

- Nicopolis (Titus 3:12)

- Possibly Spain. (The early church father Clement asserted that Paul did fulfill his desire to go Spain, expressed in Romans 15:28, but whether the visit actually took place is still uncertain.)

Eventually, Paul went back Rome, either voluntarily or involuntarily. It has been suggested that Paul had been arrested while in Nicopolis, but the evidence is uncertain. What we do know is that by the time Paul returned to Rome, the widespread persecution of Christians by the Roman emperor Nero had already begun. It's entirely possible that by this time, the apostle Peter had already been martyred in Rome, possibly being crucified upside down.

Paul's imprisonment this time was not a house arrest. Rather, it's believed to have been in the cold, infamous Mamertine Prison, where Peter might also have been held.

We do have some information about Paul's final days based on Paul's last letter to Timothy. From this very personal, heartfelt letter, we know Paul was visited by Onesiphorus, who "often refreshed me and was not ashamed of my chains" (2 Timothy

1:16–17). But we also know that Paul had been abandoned by many Christians as he faced trial (4:10, 16). Luke alone was still with Paul, although Paul expressed the hope that he would see John Mark again when Timothy came to visit (4:11).

Historical evidence agrees that Paul was executed by Nero in Rome, probably by beheading, sometime between AD 66–68. But that did not put an end to Paul's ministry. Through his letters in the New Testament, Paul still ministers to us today. Throughout the latter thirty years of his life, Paul courageously faced his God-given mission to proclaim the gospel of new and eternal life in Christ Jesus the Savior.

Mamertine Prison, as seen today, is the site where Paul (and possibly Peter) was imprisoned in Rome. Prisoners here awaited trial or execution; however, many died of diseases and starvation while held. By the eighth century AD, the site was used as a place of Christian worship.

Live It

That Paul would proclaim the gospel wasn't the only prophecy given to Ananias about Paul in Acts 9. Look at verse 16: "I [the Lord] will show [Paul] how much he must suffer for my name." Paul knew that hardship for the sake of Jesus awaited him. The Lord had chosen him and Paul had chosen to go wherever the Lord would lead, even when that path led to suffering.

While in prison, facing imminent death, Paul learned to be content and joyful in his circumstances because of the peace he had through Christ. He knew—and could reassure the church in Philippi—that "my God will meet all your needs according to the riches of his glory in Christ Jesus" (Philippians 4:19).

We can trust God to take care of all our needs and to fulfill the work to which he has called each of us. Along with Paul, we too have the opportunity to say, "I have fought the good fight, I have finished the race, I have kept the faith" (2 Timothy 4:7).

"For to me, to live is Christ and to die is gain."

PHILIPPIANS 1:21

Life Application Questions

1. If, like Paul, we're following God's calling for our lives, why might God allow us to experience some hardships and suffering?

2. What can we do to find contentment—and even joy— during times of suffering, instead of anger and bitterness?

3. When have you gone through a tough time and later been able to look back and say, "*Now* I see what God was doing through that!"

4. How can you encourage others in their circumstances right now, no matter what circumstances you're currently facing—or maybe even *through* those circumstances?

5. In Philippians, Paul writes, "I am torn between the two: I desire to depart and be with Christ, which is better by far; but it is more necessary for you that I remain in the body" (1:23–24). Have you ever felt like this? How did you respond to those conflicted feelings?

6. As we come to the end of this study, what has impressed you most deeply about Paul and what God did through his life? What might this mean for your spiritual journey?

Prayer

Dear gracious Father, thank you for all the gifts you give us. Thank you for the example of Paul—who was just a man, but a man who knew *you,* and because of that was able to accomplish great things for your kingdom. Help us remember your love and peace as we carry out our daily tasks, both big and small. Fill us with your joy and contentment as we work to carry out the purpose you have for each of our lives. In Jesus' name, amen.

This Coming Week

Consider the following options for living out your faith in response to this session's study—or come up with one of your own. Then, *do it.*

- Encourage someone, not just with your words, but also with your actions. Take a pot of soup to someone who is sick. Take a couple of bags of groceries or a gift card to someone who is struggling financially.

- Is there a friend or co-worker facing a difficult choice or circumstance? Pray for that person and let him or her *know* you're praying. If it's appropriate, put that person in touch with other Christians who have the gifts and talents to help. It would build both sides up—and probably be a pleasant surprise for both as well.

Notes

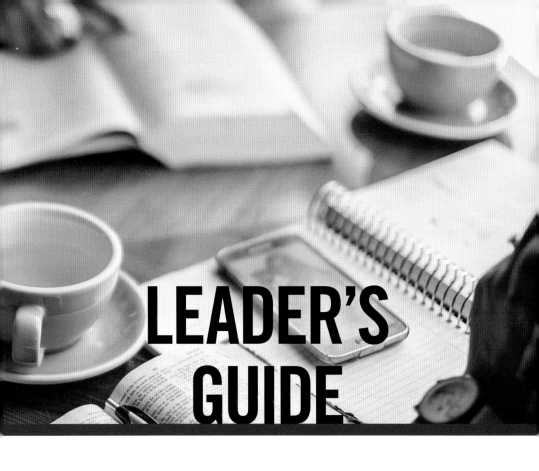

LEADER'S GUIDE

"Encourage one another
and build each other up."

1 THESSALONIANS 5:11

Leader's Guide

Congratulations! You've either decided to lead a Bible study, or you're thinking hard about it. Guess what? God does big things through small groups. When his people gather together, open his Word, and invite his Spirit to work, their lives are changed!

Do you feel intimidated yet?

Be comforted by this: even the great apostle Paul felt "in over his head" at times. When he went to Corinth to help people grasp God's truth, he admitted he was overwhelmed: "I came to you in weakness with great fear and trembling" (1 Corinthians 2:3). Later he wondered, "Who is adequate for such a task as this?" (2 Corinthians 2:16 NLT).

Feelings of inadequacy are normal; every leader has them. What's more, they're actually healthy. They keep us dependent on the Lord. It is in our times of greatest weakness that God works most powerfully. The Lord assured Paul, "My grace is sufficient for you, for my power is made perfect in weakness" (2 Corinthians 12:9).

The Goal

What is the goal of a Bible study group? Listen as the apostle Paul speaks to Christians:

- "Oh, my dear children! I feel as if I'm going through labor pains for you again, and they will continue until *Christ is fully developed in your lives*" (Galatians 4:19 NLT, emphasis added).

- "For God knew his people in advance, and he chose them *to become like his Son*" (Romans 8:29 NLT, emphasis added).

Do you see it? God's ultimate goal for us is that we would become like Jesus Christ. This means a Bible study is not about filling our heads with more information. Rather, it is about undergoing transformation. We study and apply God's truth so that it will reshape our hearts and minds, and so that, over time we will become more and more like Jesus.

Paul said, "The purpose of my instruction is that all believers would be filled with love that comes from a pure heart, a clear conscience, and genuine faith" (1 Timothy 1:5 NLT).

This isn't about trying to "master the Bible." No, we're praying that God's Word will master us, and through humble submission to its authority, we'll be changed from the inside out.

Your Role

Many group leaders experience frustration because they confuse their role with God's role. Here's the truth: God alone knows our deep hang-ups and hurts. Only he can save a soul, heal a heart, fix a life. It is God who rescues people from depression, addictions, bitterness, guilt, and shame. We Bible study leaders need to realize that *we can't do any of those things.*

So what can we do? More than we think!

- We can pray.

- We can trust God to work powerfully.

- We can obey the Spirit's promptings.

- We can prepare for group gatherings.

- We can keep showing up faithfully.

With group members:

- We can invite, remind, encourage, and love.

- We can ask good questions and then listen attentively.

- We can gently speak tough truths.

- We can celebrate with those who are happy and weep with those who are sad.

- We can call and text and let them know we've got their back.

But we can never do the things that only the Almighty can do.

- We can't play the Holy Spirit in another person's life.

- We can't be in charge of outcomes.

- We can't force God to work according to our timetables.

And one more important reminder: besides God's role and our role, group members also have a key role to play in this process. If they don't show up, prepare, or open their hearts to God's transforming truth, no life change will take place. We're not called to manipulate or shame, pressure or arm twist. We're not to blame if members don't make progress—and we don't get the credit when they do. We're mere instruments in the hands of God.

"I planted the seed, [another] watered it, but God has been making it grow. So neither the one who plants nor the one who waters is anything, but only God, who makes things grow."

1 CORINTHIANS 3:6–7

Leader Myths and Truths

Many people assume that a Bible study leader should:

- Be a Bible scholar.

- Be a dynamic communicator.

- Have a big, fancy house to meet in.

- Have it all together—no doubts, bad habits, or struggles.

These are myths—even outright lies of the enemy!

Here's the truth:

- God is looking for humble Bible students, not scholars.

- You're not signing up to give lectures, you're agreeing to facilitate discussions.

- You don't need a palace, just a place where you can have uninterrupted discussions. (Perhaps one of your group members will agree to host your study.)

- Nobody has it all together. We are all in process. We are all seeking to work out "our salvation with fear and trembling" (Philippians 2:12).

As long as your desire is that Jesus be Lord of your life, God will use you!

Some Bad Reasons to Lead a Group

- You want to wow others with your biblical knowledge.

  "Love . . . does not boast, it is not proud"
  (1 Corinthians 13:4).

- You're seeking a hidden personal gain or profit.

  "We do not peddle the word of God for profit"
  (2 Corinthians 2:17).

- You want to tell people how wrong they are.

  "Do not condemn" (Romans 2:1).

- You want to fix or rescue people.

  "It is God who works in you to will and to act"
  (Philippians 2:13).

- You're being pressured to do it.

  "Am I now trying to win the approval of
  human beings, or of God?" (Galatians 1:10).

A Few Do's

✔ Pray for your group.

Are you praying for your group members regularly? It is the most important thing a leader can do for his or her group.

✔ Ask for help.

If you're new at leading, spend time with an experienced group leader and pick his or her brain.

✔ Encourage members to prepare.

Challenge participants to read the Bible passages and the material in their study guides, and to answer and reflect on the study questions during the week prior to meeting.

✔ Discuss the group guidelines.

Go over important guidelines with your group at the first session, and again as needed if new members join the group in later sessions. See the *Group Guidelines* at the end of this leader's guide.

✔ Share the load.

Don't be a one-person show. Ask for volunteers. Let group members host the meeting, arrange for snacks, plan socials, lead group prayer times, and so forth. The old saying is true: Participants become boosters; spectators become critics.

✔ Be flexible.

If a group member shows up in crisis, it is okay to stop and take time to surround the hurting brother or sister with love. Provide a safe place for sharing. Listen and pray for his or her needs.

✔ Be kind.

Remember, there's a story—often a heart-breaking one—behind every face. This doesn't *excuse* bad or disruptive behavior on the part of group members, but it might *explain* it.

A Few Don'ts

✘ Don't "wing it."

Although these sessions are designed to require minimum preparation, read each one ahead of time. Highlight the questions you feel are especially important for your group to spend time on.

✘ Don't feel ashamed to say, "I don't know."

Disciple means "learner," not "know-it-all."

✘ Don't feel the need to "dump the truck."

You don't have to say everything you know. There is always next week. A little silence during group discussion time, that's fine. Let members wrestle with questions.

✘ Don't put members on the spot.

Invite others to share and pray, but don't pressure them. Give everyone an opportunity to participate. People will open up on their own time as they learn to trust the group.

✘ Don't go down "rabbit trails."

Be careful not to let one person dominate the time or for the discussion to go down the gossip road. At the same time, don't short-circuit those occasions when the Holy Spirit is working in your group members' lives and therefore they *need* to share a lot.

✘ Don't feel pressure to cover every question.

Better to have a robust discussion of four questions than a superficial conversation of ten.

✘ Don't go long.

Encourage good discussion, but don't be afraid to "rope 'em back in" when needed. Start and end on time. If you do this from the beginning, you'll avoid the tendency of group members to arrive later and later as the season goes on.

How to Use This Study Guide

Many group members have busy lives—dealing with long work hours, childcare, and a host of other obligations. These sessions are designed to be as simple and straightforward as possible to fit into a busy schedule. Nevertheless, encourage group members to set aside some time during the week (even if it's only a little) to pray, read the key Bible passage, and respond to questions in this study guide. This will make the group discussion and experience much more rewarding for everyone.

Each session contains four parts.

Read It

The *Key Bible Passage* is the portion of Scripture everyone should read during the week before the group meeting. The group can read it together at the beginning of the session as well.

The *Optional Reading* is for those who want to dig deeper and read lengthier Bible passages on their own during the week.

Know It

This section encourages participants to reflect on the Bible passage they've just read. Here, the goal is to interact with the biblical text and grasp what it says. (We'll get into practical application later.)

Explore It

Here group members can find background information with charts and visuals to help them understand the Bible passage and the topic more deeply. They'll move beyond the text itself and see how it connects to other parts of Scripture and the historical and cultural context.

Live It

Finally, participants will examine how God's Word connects to their lives. There are application questions for group discussion or personal reflection, practical ideas to apply what they've learned from God's Word, and a closing thought and/or prayer. (Remember, you don't have to cover all the questions or everything in this section during group time. Focus on what's most important for your group.)

Celebrate!

Here's an idea: Have a plan for celebrating your time together after the last session of this Bible study. Do something special after your gathering time, or plan a separate celebration for another time and place. Maybe someone in your group has the gift of hospitality—let them use their gifting and organize the celebration.

	30-MINUTE SESSION	60-MINUTE SESSION
READ IT	Open in prayer and read the *Key Bible Passage.* 5 minutes	Open in prayer and read the *Key Bible Passage.* 5 minutes
KNOW IT	Ask: "What stood out to you from this Bible passage?" 5 minutes	Ask: "What stood out to you from this Bible passage?" 5 minutes
EXPLORE IT	Encourage group members to read this section on their own, but don't spend group time on it. Move on to the life application questions.	Ask: "What did you find new or helpful in the *Explore It* section? What do you still have questions about?" 10 minutes
LIVE IT	Members voluntarily share their answers to 3 or 4 of the life application questions. 15 minutes	Members voluntarily share their answers to the life application questions. 25 minutes
PRAYER & CLOSING	Conclude with a brief prayer. 5 minutes	Share prayer requests and praise reports. Encourage the group to pray for each other in the coming week. Conclude with a brief prayer. 15 minutes

Open in prayer and read the *Key Bible Passage.*

5 minutes

- Ask: "What stood out to you from this Bible passage?"
- Then go over the *Know It* questions as a group.

10 minutes

- Ask: "What did you find new or helpful in the *Explore It* section? What do you still have questions about?"
- Here, the leader can add information found while preparing for the session.
- If there are questions or a worksheet in this section, go over those as a group.

20 minutes

- Members voluntarily share their answers to the life application questions.
- Wrap up this time with a closing thought or suggestions for how to put into practice in the coming week what was just learned from God's Word.

30 minutes

- Share prayer requests and praise reports.
- Members voluntarily pray during group time about the requests and praises shared.
- Encourage the group to pray for each other in the coming week.

25 minutes

Group Guidelines

This group is about discovering God's truth, supporting each other, and finding growth in our new life in Christ. To reach these goals, a group needs a few simple guidelines that everyone should follow for the group to stay healthy and for trust to develop.

1. **Everyone agrees to make group time a priority.**
   We understand that there are work, health, and family issues that come up. So if there is an emergency or schedule conflict that cannot be avoided, be sure to let someone know that you can't make it that week. This may seem like a small thing, but it makes a big difference to your other group members.

2. **What is said in the group stays in the group.**
   Accept it now: we are going to share some personal things. Therefore, the group must be a safe and confidential place to share.

3. **Don't be judgmental, even if you strongly disagree.**
   Listen first, and contribute your perspective only as needed. Remember, you don't fully know someone else's story. Take this advice from James: "Be quick to listen, slow to speak, and slow to become angry" (James 1:19).

4. **Be patient with one another.**
   We are all in process, and some of us are hurting and struggling more than others. Don't expect bad habits or attitudes to disappear overnight.

5. **Everyone participates.**
   It may take time to learn how to share, but as you develop a trust toward the other group members, take the chance.

If you struggle in any of these areas, ask God's help for growth, and ask the group to help hold you accountable. Remember, you're all growing together.

Notes

ROSE VISUAL BIBLE STUDIES
6-Session Study Guides for Personal or Group Use

Rose Visual Bible Studies are packed with full-color visuals that show key information at a glance! With their easy-to-use format—*read it*, *know it*, *explore it*, and *live it*—these 6-week inductive studies are perfect for gaining a deeper insight into God's Word.

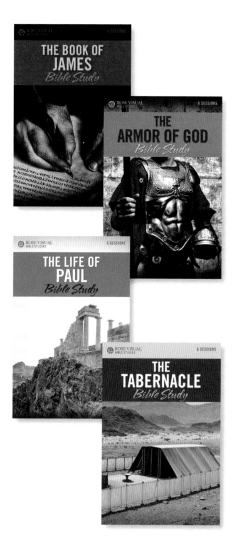

THE BOOK OF JAMES
Find out what James says about cultivating a genuine living faith through six tests of faith: trials, favoritism, good works, speech, relationships, and prayer.
ISBN 9781628627589

THE ARMOR OF GOD
Dig deep into Ephesians 6 and learn the meaning of each piece of the armor, its historical uses, and its application to spiritual battles today.
ISBN 9781628627558

THE LIFE OF PAUL
From his conversion on the road to Damascus to his martyrdom in Rome, see how the apostle Paul persevered through trials and fearlessly proclaimed the gospel of Jesus.
ISBN 9781628627619

THE TABERNACLE
From the golden lampstand to the ark of the covenant, discover how each item of the tabernacle foreshadowed Jesus and what that means for us today.
ISBN 9781628627527

HENDRICKSON PUBLISHERS   ROSE PUBLISHING

www.hendricksonrose.com